# What Is God?

# JOSEPH F. GIRZONE

*Doubleday*

NEW YORK   LONDON

TORONTO   SYDNEY   AUCKLAND

# What Is God?

PUBLISHED BY DOUBLEDAY
a division of Bantam Doubleday Dell Publishing Group, Inc.
1540 Broadway, New York, New York 10036

DOUBLEDAY and the portrayal of an anchor with a dolphin are
trademarks of Doubleday, a division of Bantam Doubleday Dell
Publishing Group, Inc.

Book design by Jennifer Ann Daddio
Illustrations by Leslie Wu

Library of Congress Cataloging-in-Publication Data
Girzone, Joseph F.
What is God?/Joseph F. Girzone
p.  cm.
1. God    I. Title
BT102.G55  1996
231'.4—dc20      96-23179
CIP
AC

ISBN 0-385-48261-2

# FOREWORD

*Late one evening as I was walking through my garden before retiring, I was struck with an awareness of God that momentarily stunned me. It was so simple yet so profound. I saw in the briefest moment how God is in every part of creation all at one time, and knows every detail of creation in an instant, like the rays of the rising sun touching everything in a single moment, knowing every expression of joy, and every cry of pain from the human heart individually at once, so simply. This intimate awareness of God's presence was so clear I wanted never to forget it. Not trusting my memory, as soon as I went into the house I sat down and tried to put on paper what I had experienced in that brief moment. It was difficult analyzing the experience and breaking it down into individual thoughts. It took me over an hour to describe what I had experienced in an instant. When I finished I realized how inadequate it was. But it was the best I could do.*

*From that night on I saw God differently. "In Him we live and move and have our being" made sense. God is not far from any one of us. In Him we live and flourish. Indeed, He is in everything around us, not that everything is God, but His presence is there, sustaining us in existence, with a love and tenderness that is ineffable, with a gentle understanding of our fragile weakness that can put to rest any fear of Him. His love and understanding of our humanness is overwhelming, far beyond our ability to comprehend. We are His and He loves us as He made us and is with us as we walk through life, gently growing into His reflection.*

*This beautiful thought of God has been for me a treasured blessing, and I am happy to share this treasure with you, my friends.*

JOSEPH F. GIRZONE

# What Is God?

*God is the beauty*

*in a little wildflower.*

God *is fragrance in a delicate rose, music in a mountain brook.*

*God is life in the earth that gives renewal to all creation in the springtime.*

God is warm rays of sun in winter,

radiant beauty in new-fallen snow,

and the pattern in a geometrically designed snowflake.

God is the timelessness

of the waters

that carved out

the history of time

in the Grand Canyon.

*God* is the immense power

*of the ocean and the infinite expanse of space,*

*the speed in a ray of light traveling from a golden sunrise,*

*the light of the universe,*

*and the order holding all creation in its ever-moving course.*

God is the dignified majesty

in a towering spruce,

the mightiness in a giant sequoia,

and the fire in the orange and red leaves

in nature's autumn masterpiece.

God is the life in all living things

and the uniqueness of each individual

of every species of plant and animal—

the naïveté of a deer,

the unrelenting faithfulness of a sheepdog,

the playfulness of a kitten,

the comedy in a giraffe,

the simplicity in a dove,

and the craftiness in a fox.

God is the beauty in a blue sky

and the motion in a feathery cloud

floating across the vast airy ocean.

God *is the humor in the frost playing games*

*on a windowpane on a cold winter morning,*

*and the dancing life in a warming fire.*

*God* is the tenderness of a mother's love, the security of a father's

spirit in an artist's fingers, the music in a composer's soul, and the lyricism

the inventor, the healing power in a doctor's hands, the courage of a lonely

*strength, and the refreshing honesty of a child's mind. God is the creative*

*in a poet's pen. God is the vision of the prophet, the discoverer and*

*soldier on a battlefield, and the sacredness of a holy man offering sacrifice.*

God is the trinity in the light

and the warmth of the sun;

the Son, the Spirit, and the Father all in one.

*God is the magnificence*

*of a sunset.*

$God$ is the love that thrills the human heart,

the joy of friendship,

and the cheer in a carefree laugh.

God is all the colors of the spectrum blending

into pure white light.

God is the air we breathe and the color we see;

the music we hear and the fragrance we smell

and the sweetness we taste.

$God$ is the very life that courses through the human soul.

violate the integrity of their own mind or be deaf to the voices

*And if someone says they cannot see God in all of this, they must either*

*of all creation that cry out so loudly from the womb of the universe.*

# ABOUT THE AUTHOR

*Father Joseph Girzone retired from the active priesthood for health reasons, and then embarked on the surprising writing career that has brought him millions of readers and admirers. Among his bestselling titles are* Joshua *and* Never Alone: A Personal Way to God. *He lives in Altamont, New York.*

# ABOUT THE ILLUSTRATOR

*Leslie Wu is an artist whose works have been widely exhibited and are held in many collections in the United States and in Japan. She lives in Rochester, New York, with her husband and daughter.*